DEDICATION

This second edition is dedicated to my valued mentors, in particular

Kazuo Matsuzaki
Hans Went
Giorgio Lupi
Valerian Lupi
Paul Steczkowicz
Arthur Rowe
Gary Jackson

The LITTLE RED SUCCESS BOOK

Third Edition published by
Easy Online Portals Pty Ltd
GPO Box 865
Brisbane 4001 Australia

Enquiries to Information@easyonlineportals.com

Cover Design by PIXEL PRODUCTIONS

First Edition Printed by Broderick Printing and Design Limited
Auckland New Zealand

Second Edition Released as electronic version April 2009

ISBN 0-473-02585-X

INDEX

Authors Note:

The quotations on the title pages are the result of
translation and interpretation by a friend who is a Chinese Scholar,
and the Author.

The characters used in Tao Te Ching, by Lao Tzu, are very traditional
and do not translate easily into simple, modern day English. With
my friend's translation skills and my English comprehension we have
spent many hours, before agreement was reached.

We had to reach a compromise between easily understood meaning
and pure translation. Sadly, much of the poetic beauty of Lao Tzu's
work has been negated to ensure the simplicity of this book remained
intact.

FOREWORD

Originally this book was written for a few friends who had asked me questions about success and happiness. Success and happiness go hand in hand, and as one of my valued mentors once said:
'Neither can exist without the other'

When I challenged his statement he explained that a successful person in business must also be happy in their private life, or the corporate success would only be a passing moment. He said that for a person to be truly successful they must be round, and complete, like a concentric circle - growing, knowing the direction and remaining always rounded. It was a tough philosophy for a 20 year old to accept, but after many years of study on many planes, I believe he was right.

Throughout my life, I have been able to attract many powerful, motivating people into my life and they have contributed infinitely to my growth. Sometimes in ignorance I fought them, and only in later life have I understood how much faster I could have been where I wanted to go if I had been open and willing to respond to their lessons earlier. This book, now that I was convinced to publish it for others to read, is dedicated to some of those mentors.

How do we judge whether we are successful or not?

We need to answer two questions:

1.   How much of your time do you feel really happy?
2.   How many of the goals, tasks or ideas that you have set yourself have you achieved?
If your answer to both these questions is above 90%, then you already have the answers and you don't really need this book.

This book is designed to be easy to read, and is written in everyday conversational English. Take it along with you and learn how to be successful and happy.

It is simple, very simple, but not necessarily easy - it depends on you and how much you want it. I can only explain how. No-one but you can do it for you! Did you know that actually no one else can determine, or even influence, your happiness or success unless you allow them to?

We are now going to leave **APATHY** behind and embrace **ARPIFEE** instead. Enjoy the experience! I hope to meet you one day.

With Love,
Terrie

PROLOGUE

There are many teachers and leaders of what is often termed 'new age' philosophy, but I have found evidence of similar teachings even in the period BC, so this is not new, but just lost in the whirlwind of our everyday lives. Most of the teachers have selected a part of the philosophy, or a state, in which to specialise. This text is aimed at the difficult, often transitional period, through which we must progress. The earthly physical culture, controlled by the 'collective mind' [1] through into the metaphysical philosophies that teach you control, of your attitude to life, through the flow of energy and power of natural, universal law.

There are no University degrees in Human Empowerment, so how do you have any way of establishing my credibility to discuss these topics?

First let me answer the two questions I raised in the foreward:
'How much of your time do you feel really happy?' My Answer is 98%,
'How many of the goals, tasks or ideas that you have set, or accepted yourself have you achieved?' My answer is 100% - Honestly.

I ask myself these questions every few months, and for nearly 20 years my answers have been pretty much the same.

I made a commitment between 1980 and 1990 to study

between 20 and 60 hours per week with other teachers, and researched texts both modern and ancient. I attended all sorts of seminars, meetings and one on one consultations to see what worked and what didn't. In 2009, I still spend a couple of hours every day reviewing and researching new material for any additional information, and reaffirming my own practices.

Probably the most important credential is the fact that I do use these teachings as a lifestyle still today, and do not enforce my beliefs on others, even those in the same household. I am very comfortable with the cause and effect of the information and programme in this book. I believe every teacher must continue to live their teachings as a daily example, or else they risk losing their credibility.

If I cannot, or have not, done the things that I recommend you do, then my own credibility is at risk.

It is through living these teachings as a lifestyle that I continue to achieve the goals I set myself, or accept from others. This also helps me sustain an inner peace and experience self-confidence and happiness.

Beyond the simple lessons in this book, there are many wise and wonderful teachers who will continue to assist you to seek greater knowledge, and more specialised skills in other facets such as healing, vision and leadership. You won't have to struggle to find them, they will be there when you need them.

My mission is to reach as many people as possible with Little Red Success Book, touch their lives and hopefully inspire them to desire what is available to them. The purpose is to assist with the first confusing, sometimes a little overwhelming, steps on the pathway to success and happiness.

Overall, success is a fairly easy thing to obtain and probably 10-15% of the population would be considered fairly successful, but the combination with a very high level of satisfaction and happiness seems to be the elusive part.

I surveyed some friends recently and could not find anyone who could unconditionally state they were happy That was a big shock for me.

Many of them had conditional happiness - i.e. "I'll be happy when I
get something, or some situation occurs".

One person replied, "Exactly which part of my life do you want to know about?" When I explained I meant totally happy, I was received with cynical humour, "Are you crazy? Of course not, but I am happy with my social life, I just hate my job and I suffer from migraines." Then he went on to name 14 other unhappiness factors. At the end of all this, he stopped and asked me half jokingly, "Is anyone ever totally happy? I doubt it' he said- 'it isn't really possible, there is always something wrong!"

My response was "Yes, I am totally happy. "
I know I was not believed.

What has happened to cause people to feel that a state of mind, equal to total happiness, which I believe is everyone's right, can be impossible to achieve?

I want to briefly touch upon the "collective mind" as it is an important aspect for you to understand. The collective mind is the culture, traditions and expectations of our society. There are a squillion things we do and think every day, that are controlled and influenced by the collective mind.

My Mother has always talked of the things "you must do".
To give you an example, a family gathering occurs such as a wedding or funeral, and you really don't want to go, but you feel you "must" - that is the control and influence of the "collective mind".
It is one of the greatest causes of unhappiness in anyone of enquiring mind. The collective mind can be a comfortable place, it helps the masses - but you would scoff at, not purchase, this book if you were happy to be of the masses. As a result you have chosen to break out of the collective mind and forge your own unique path up the mountain to your source.

Who, or what is the Source? Whoever feels right for you - God, God-force, the Universe, Buddha whatever you need to call the supreme source of energy. For non-denominational, and non-discrimination reasons, I shall call it just the Source - it is from where I came and it is where I shall return when the time is right. There is no need for anyone following this book to need a religion; if you have one and you are happy then this book will fit in with it. If you are an atheist or agnostic, the book also works, these principles are not discriminatory at all.

The set of laws governing all life and nature, has always and will continue to be called Universal Law, or natural law. This controls everything - the movement of galaxies to the birth cycle of a gnat, and comes from the Source. We learn eventually to flow with this amazing energy and use it to fulfill our needs. To be in harmony with natural universal law is to have a very inspirational and highly evolved life.

This text is just the beginning - from the first question of how to be happier, through to a point of embarking on a quest for great knowledge and understanding. This is the kindergarten to prepare you to accept the real thing.

It is amazing that nature has this knowledge in-built but we humans, because of our collective mind conditioning from birth, must begin again to learn the basic knowledge.

I know from experience if you can see these lessons through, you will have received a very special gift of vision. In addition, you will have rewarded me with another step closer to my goals.

ANALYSE

A journey of a thousand miles begins with one step

.... Interpretation from Tao Te Ching.

Analyse

Before we can achieve success and happiness we have to take some time to look within at what we have. This may take some time - my suggestion is to read through the book and then come back here and start again.

I first considered truly analysing myself on my 30th birthday. I had been very successful in my business life, but I was unhappy within.

Analysis of oneself takes enormous courage and conviction - be warned you may not like what you find, and some things may seem overwhelming. My advice now is to remember the old adage "How do you eat an elephant? A small piece at a time."

OK, how do we go about this analysis? First of all, take a quiet hour or so when you feel calm and unhurried. Take a sheet of paper, divide it into two and write down the things you know about yourself - put on the left the things you feel are negative and on the right the positive ones. Be honest, no one else need ever see this paper. Assess your personality, but also the physical aspects of your life and look for imbalance. Consider your environment, your work, your diet, sleep patterns and leisure activities

If you drink too much alcohol, need dope, eat poorly or only eat convenience pre-packaged food, exercise minimally then you need to adjust and address that. Usually people booze, smoke (whatever), "trip", over-eat, over-spend or slob, dress poorly because they feel unhappy, discontented or don't love themselves. These physical up-potions become addictive and replace true deep happiness, and blow success right out of the probable. Some people even go as far as despising symbols of happiness or success. Ever hear a sad person growl ' What are you smiling for anyway?' I have!

Secondly you can ask a few people how they see you. This takes guts, and you must never speak when they tell you.
Never speak, for the first time in your life, shut up and truly listen - pretend they are talking about something else if it helps. I carried a block of wood and put it on the table and said "Imagine that's me, tell me what you see?" It was easier to remain objective from the personal emotion this way.

There are key points to remember to make this part of the exercise effective:

1. Their perception may be wrong, or it may not.

2. You must listen very carefully and understand what they mean, not just what they say.

3. Be aware it is tougher on them than you - so don't spring it on them. Make an   appointment for 15 minutes of their time. No more, no less.

4. Choose people who know you for different reasons and lengths of time - include people who have known you only recently. *You will need about five or six impressions, For example you could choose*

from your spouse, children (even if they are small, they can be very insightful), parents, siblings, employer, work colleague, best friend and someone you met quite recently who inspired you.

5. Write it all down so you can reflect on it later.

6. Make no decisions, do nothing until you have completed your research.

7. Take about three hours alone and bring your lists. On a large sheet of paper (or a whiteboard) divided into squares, write the key points from each person. Then use a hi-liter and mark the common threads in each individual observation - these traits, good or bad, will illustrate the 'real you' unchanged by external influences. In another colour, mark any particular traits anywhere that concern you.

8. Compare this analysis with what you wrote - again highlighting the common points and those that concern you.   *How well did you analyse yourself? Were you really honest? If you were, there will be no surprises. Forget everything else on all the lists + or - as they probably don't matter anymore at this stage.*

9. Then write up ALL the positive points from every list and pin it up on the wall where you can see it night and morning. Say them to yourself, preferably aloud. It will reinforce your love for yourself. After a while try adding "Your name, I love you!", at the end of the list. This will increase your current

happiness level by a large percentage, even if you do no more ever!

10. Make up a second list of the negative points, preferably on red pieces of paper and clip them together safely.

So now you have analysed yourself - is there a lot you want to change?

If there is, then this analysis will become a dynamic exercise and need repeating every six months or so. If there is little to change, then you are well on your way already.

Don't be horrified if there is a lot you want to change - my list was so long it took me three years to work through the bulk of it, and another six years to face the three or four really tough, well practised ones!

Nine years of commitment to my own self development, and I will always have to run a little check now and then to see how it is - old, bad habits like to sneak back if you allow them. I do it, if I feel negative, emotional or unhappy for more than an hour - I check and see "who" has sneaked in the back door and kick them out! (It is usually Mr. Judgment!)

Nine years was a long time, but I was not well focused and I kept thinking it was too hard – the old three steps forward and two-four back routine! All I can tell you now, it was totally, absolutely and completely worth it.

It feels so good today, I can't believe I gave up so many times. With this Little Red Book to guide you, it will be so much easier!

As I said earlier it is a simple message, but not an easy path. Climbing the highest mountain is tough, requires considerable pre-planning and effort but the result is worth it - then you forget the blisters, bruises, trauma and cold just reveling in the wonder and brilliance of achievement and perspective.

OK, so you've got this red list, what do you do with it?

Eat it, metaphorically speaking, piece by piece.

Assess how large and deep rooted each item is – can you do it alone? How long has it been there? Who can help?

Lots of people, places and things can help. It is not possible in this book, as its mission is simplicity, to cover this topic - it would be a book in itself.

However, to assist you I have put a list in the back outlining some material you could consider and see what feels right for you - read about each facet and decide for yourself. It is a case of trial and error. In addition, you will find the rest of the things in this little book will help

Understand that as you begin to feel happier you will be on a higher plane metaphysically, so when the darker moments come you have further to fall and further to climb - so it hurts more! The old courage is needed again. The only consolation I can offer you is that after a few decent falls, you begin to know the way up better and faster!

Do you have the courage and conviction to keep reading? All I can do is promise that although your path may be rough and rocky, there is a pot of gold at the end!

Every day of the rest of your life can feel pretty amazing and wonderfully fulfilled once you think and act in accordance with what many call the Seven Secrets of Success! These are the principles in this book.

■

Key Notes - Analyse

Analysis of oneself takes enormous courage and conviction.

Other people's perception may be right, or it may not.

This step is essential to identify the habits that need to change to allow you to be happy

REFLECT

Talking excessively will lead to emptiness. Retain balance and harmony

.... Interpretation from Tao Te Ching.

Reflect

If you are still reading, that is exciting and we can enter stage two together.

The world is a tumultuous place, sometimes seeming wonderful and sometimes like a bucket of sewerage. Reflection is the art of being able to step back and away metaphysically and view everything from an objective perspective.

If today you are struggling in a bucket of sewerage, it is hard to think while you are swimming around trying to stay alive. The nice thing about reflection, is that it is peaceful, calming and free. It is also alone, but now that you understand yourself better, that won't be so tough. It is nice to spend time with yourself, when you like yourself, as you become your own best friend.

We have to step out of the hustle, and begin to feel the inner peace. In the early stages this can be really simple stuff - just go to your favourite nearby place where you can be mentally alone. A park, a temple, beach, dockside, cliff top, your deck, apartment, even your office (press DND on the phone).

Sit comfortably, spine straight, feet apart - close your eyes, breath in deeply and slowly, hold a few seconds, exhale deeply and slowly - three times is good. Then think of your toes, wiggle them, feel them on an outward breath, relax them. Progress on up your body, until you complete the procedure with your scalp.

You will realise now that for the last ten minutes you have forgotten everything but yourself - great! You will already feel more in control, less emotional, better. This is called *centering* it is relaxing, self-controlling and disciplined.

Once you are centered then you have a choice. You can simply meditate or you can reflect upon one particular aspect, calmly, without emotion or involvement. The white light of clarity will shine upon your aspect and you will be able to study it, move it, turn it, size it and probably solve your attitude to it. Just like the block of wood that was you in phase one.

First of all look at each situation differently, study it in minute detail – how big is it?
Will you remember it this time tomorrow, next week, next month, next year?
Will it devastate your life? (Unlikely event, unless you let it!) or does it just hurt now?
Can you pluck it out like an arrow, or do you need to consult a healer?
What is your immediate step toward healing (one piece at a time)? If it's huge, take this first immediate step then reflect again.

If you want to reflect just on whatever passes, then just focus on one thing, anything, and let the mind drift - simple meditation. If you like this feeling then learn to meditate - it is healing, calming and powerful. You can take a course, or read a book, ask someone who meditates or just practice. If you want to experience deep meditation, I believe it is best to obtain a very experienced guide to take you through the first time at least.

You also need to reflect upon your red pieces of paper, one at a time. The healing will come, then when you know you have it conquered, burn the piece ceremoniously. Preferably, with a statement like "Be gone, I am renewed", or similar words that suit your style.

Fire is important in our life, as the great purifier. It is one of the core elements of our physical life - when a fire burns untouched it leaves behind nothing, no trace of the object, just the ash of another fire.
Metaphysically this is a powerful cleanser and purifier. Not long before the completion of this little book, I went through a fire walk which was a powerful culmination to my ten years of study, practice and self development. It was, without doubt, one of the greatest moments of my life and a complete attitude changer.

Reflection must become part of your daily life. You cannot centre without reflection, and you cannot remain rational and unemotional without centering.

After a while you will be able to centre within a few minutes, almost anywhere just as you feel the spin of emotion beginning to catch you! TIME OUT - CENTRE - CONTROL - it feels just amazing.

I try to centre at least every hour or so - especially if I find myself in stressful circumstances. In the early stages, excuse yourself and go to the toilet (everyone accepts a toilet break), breathe, centre yourself and return to the situation in control.

While we are under the *Reflect* category, we need to continue to reflect regularly on how we went today physically and metaphysically. This should form a lifetime habit. I do this at night before bed and in the morning whilst showering.

At night I check up on how well I performed to my own standards today (never mind anyone else's standards, you can only live up to your own to be happy), and I never punish myself for failure – just reflect, accept and set a corrective action plan for improvement tomorrow.

In the morning I reflect only on my corrected action plan, resolutions for the day and remind myself that I do love myself - spirit and body. If you don't love yourself you won't try - it's too hard!

If I begin to sicken with any illness, I ask myself why, and use reflection to find the cause behind my body feeling ill. To understand more about this aspect of yourself, refer to the help list at the back of the book under physical healing. Who wants to pay for aspirin, when the physical characteristics are already within us to heal ourselves of daily minor complaints?

Reflect also on what your goals and your future should hold to keep you happy. These again can be on any plane, only you know what you want from this lifetime of evolutionary experience. However, one basic comment of caution here is that if your list only consists of new physical objects - reflect again, you may be missing the point and a lot of happiness.

Lasting success and happiness comes mostly from within and goes with you wherever you go, whenever you go.

It never leaves, never (unless you ask it to by word or action). If you find only physical things provide happiness and success, then you will be attached to them. What happens if someone, or something takes them away? You will be unhappy and unsuccessful as you no longer have them, you will likely try to blame someone else for your unhappiness.

Once you have established goals write them down and affirm your right to achieve them frequently. I use "I deserve ..." and "I have...". Importantly when your goal is a reality, immediately and without hesitation set the next one, otherwise your conscious mind will destroy you before you realise. A bored conscious mind with nothing to focus on, is quickly our enemy.

If your goal is enormous and far reaching, break it down into steps and revert to the "eating an elephant" philosophy and set about achieving it step by step. Do not falter or waiver, unless you no longer desire the ultimate goal you have set yourself

Generally, I have come to accept that if the happiness and success is developed within, then wherever you go and whatever you hold, you will see beauty, fascination and miracles, and you will have an abundance of whatever you need. It is unnecessary to have more than you need, everything is in abundance and it makes you no more successful or happy to have excess - surprise, surprise!!

If you are swimming in that bucket of manure, feeling ugly, or stoned off your face - will the eighth car or fourth TV make one bit of difference to how you feel or perceive yourself? Of course not, at least not more than a passing moment, before you need some other solace.

Reflection, and centering, will come to form a habit that you will carry on through your success, it will become an essential element of happiness. Lose it, and you lose your grip on the higher planes along with the vehicle to climb them.

Practise it daily, consciously, until the habit becomes a close and familiar friend.

■

Key Notes - Reflect

The nice thing about reflection is that it is peaceful, calming and free.

Fire is important in our life, it is the great purifier.

Lasting success and happiness comes from within and goes with you wherever you go, whenever you go.

PURGE

Is the higher value in title or life?
Does life or possession mean more?
Is it better to gain than to lose?
The more we hang onto anything, increases the
cost and the sense of loss,
To understand when we have enough, is to provide
safety, strength and longevity.

.... Interpretation from Tao Te Ching

Purge

It doesn't get easier - and you thought 'phase one' was challenging! Get a load of what you are about to attempt now -

Purging, like reflection, is an ongoing habitual review of circumstances. Once we have established what and who we are, where we are heading and we have learnt the art of reflective observation without emotion, we are beginning to feel somewhat different, unique and special. Who is in control of our lives now? We are - but what about all those family members and friends who need us, call upon us and stuff up our control?

This question plagued me for years, and I always found I could hold great happiness, until someone else came along and messed it up for me. I now understand that I let them mess it up. I am responsible for me, and for my reaction to whatever happens to me, no one else.

First, let's look at the needs of those around us. What do they want? An emotional crutch? Go look in a mirror - do you look like a crutch? If you do - reflect upon your humanity long and hard! I've seen human crutches - usually arthritic, shoulders slouched from the weight of the world, moving at abnormal speed, often ill, attracting poor quality luck - but everyone likes them! That is, everyone but themselves.

You know these people.

You hear about them all the time -"Did you hear about poor old Charlie - on his way home from the Church fete and had a heart attack at the wheel? Terrible. He was too good a guy. Do you know he stood there in 30 degrees all day cooking the sausage sizzle? I was only talking to him last night at the Men's Society working-bee while he was painting the ceiling - great guy, never complained, always pleasant." (No wonder he chose fast exit, stage left, heart attack - he'd had enough!)

Elsie, who raised seven kids, husband was an alcoholic, but Elsie went on to foster troubled children and was always working for this, that and everything free of charge - never took time for herself, she believed she needed only to serve others, she didn't believe she deserved anything for herself 'that was for selfish people' such a hard life, then Elsie died of cancer - everyone loved Elsie, but Elsie!

Emotional crutches are loved by many people, after all they are so useful to everyone. I am not trying to imply that we should avoid helping others, but limit the impact on our own life and **ensure we are choosing to help, not feel we have to.**

Back to you (allow me an occasional aberration!).

Your family and friends want you to join their ride! Probably, they think it is right that you only share with them and you will be happy in claustrophobic circle of demand, responsibility and their turmoil.

You get to go along on all their emotional trips with them, sharing the pain, negativity and demotivation. Sometimes you get to share the good times as well. If this is the first self-development book you've ever read, I am about to shock you, but surprisingly if you are serious about wanting success and happiness, you will discover I am neither the first, nor the last to understand purging. **You** have got to control your life, now.

Shock, horror! How?

Take these steps slowly and spend a little time thinking about what I have written.

 Ask whether it applies to you, and how you could approach your circumstances differently. Always remember, being happy is your birthright!

Step One: Analyse, Reflect & Centre

What is their rationale for wanting to control you? They may not have your commitment to development, they want to lean on your strength and sap your energy. If they are in trouble, they need their crutches. Do them a favour - analyse, reflect, centre - decide how big it really is, offer help accordingly, unemotionally, without buying their trip and without disrupting your life and boarding the train of negativity.

As a guide, if you feel resentful, emotional, critical or negative in any way, don't do anything - if you feel genuinely happy and unemotional about offering assistance, go ahead.

I am liberal with physical objects I can spare (including cash), and hugs, smiles and an ear. But I am mean with sympathy, emotion, tears, judgment, decision and agreement. No one in trouble actually benefits from any of these. They must face whatever they have attracted. I sometimes admit to people ' I am selfish' but they often reply 'No you are not' They have learnt I am there for them, as a friend or colleague, but not to be their crutch.

What if it is a death, I hear you say?
For whatever reason it was their chosen destiny.

If you analyse it, post-death sorrow is actually self pity, shock and perhaps fear and loneliness. It is natural to feel those things, but be aware evolution continues and the pain lessens if allowed to. The person who has died is not experiencing these emotions and will not cast judgment on you and your reactions. There is a short period where intense grief may cripple us, but to carry a heavy burden beyond that is damaging to our 'physmentals"[2]. After this period we should begin to look forward again and try to manage the grief into a receding phase, replaced by happy memories of the joys you shared with that person, this allows active living and a foreward movement again.

Before you write me off as a hard-nosed old woman who has obviously never felt grief (because you would be very wrong), just imagine the scenario on the following page:

2. Physmentals means the mind body interconnection.

Scenario for your contemplation:

You are with a group of friends and family walking along a busy, polluted, hot and humid, noisy city street. You feel terrible. Suddenly, just as you feel you can't go on, a clouded glass panel appears in front of you and somehow it looks inviting - you find you can step through it. On the other side you discover it is a cool, calm, refreshing forest with a lovely stream and birds singing. You can hear lovely music and see people happy and laughing on the other bank.
You feel fantastic - you turn around in amazement to discuss this phenomenon with your group - you are alone! You look behind and there you find the panel is one way reflective - your friends and family are crying and banging on the panel, begging you to come back. You are torn in half - here are the people you love, needing you to return to the hot, dirty street, in great distress, but you wonder why they won't be happy for you, because you feel wonderful. Then you realise they are ignorant – they don't know you are hoppy.
You turn away and cross
the stream, somewhat sad that your friends feel such pain, but your own joy overwhelms everything and you keep walking away.

I cannot explain what this visualisation I have just created here means to you. Only you can decide, I just hope it helps you understand that death is a part of life, and so is grief.

Some Australian Aboriginal tribes have a custom not to mention a deceased person's name again after the farewell ceremony. This is to facilitate the healing and show respect for the deceased. It is a simple and effective way for the tribe to recover and move forward.

Step Two: Analyse, Reflect and Centre

Of your circle of acquaintances, are there some negative people who always seem to drag you into their sewer bucket?

Think this through carefully, there usually are!

You could just start to gently walk away, without causing significant pain to either you or them, because if you do it well, you will be gone before they fully realise. Do not be concerned, they will not be lonely; there are plenty of victims willing to sacrifice their happiness and be dragged into the negativity of others.

Sometimes these people cannot be purged physically without hurting others, for example in-laws (because your spouse will be hurt and that would make you unhappy).

In these cases, you can be in their presence and spend the time with regular moments of centering, - staying calm, detached, unemotional but surprisingly pleasant. I go into a first stage of meditation and only speak when spoken to, but appear happy and relaxed.

For example, when I am asked my opinion of Auntie Flo's new husband, I stick to neutral answers like "the main thing is that Aunty Flo is happy" etc.
This will diffuse any situation and place these people in a state of confusion unable to effectively attack. If they

throw spears (verbal attacks or negativity) I say "thank you", or "that's interesting" - formidable ammunition, try it.

It is hard for them to keep going, imagine:

'You are not very smart'
'That is an interesting statement, why do you say that?'
'You did so many stupid things, and you will never amount to anything'
'OK, thanks for the input'
'What do you mean thanks, is that all you have to say?'
'Pretty much, how is your job going?'

You have deflected them, now wash all the negativity out of your mind, you do not need their opinion anyway. Only you have to believe in you.

If you cannot be in someone's presence detached and centered, and they have a negative impact on you, then you must stay away no matter what the consequences.

This technique also applies to places and things that annoy you.

Step Three: Analyse, Reflect and Centre

Does anyone control you? If you have debt that cannot easily be repaid, a boss that reduces you to a wreck, or regularly find yourself in situations you don't want to be in - then you are being controlled.

It must stop, before you can feel truly happy and successful.

You must be in control of your life to feel good. If you are heavily in debt, or in a job you hate, start a plan NOW to get out of it. Write it down and stick to it, no matter what. Automatically, you will feel better anyway, even though you still have to physically be there now. No one can insist that you metaphysically have to suffer, your spirit is free to come and go whenever you want!

In these situations I use creative visualisation and affirmations so that my spirit immediately begins to feel the rewards of not being there, in that place. Once you can do this, nothing will be denied!
Try using "I deserve a wonderful new job" or "I deserve $25,000 in the bank" as affirmations.

However, a word of caution. Don't just daydream and expect - daydreaming won't be enough. Increase your energy, appreciate the benefits of your present position and make the best of what you have while you're waiting. All of this positive energy will begin to attract the results you want. Visualise how you will be when your circumstances change. Please note, use the word 'when' not 'if'

If it is debt controlling you - make a plan and stick to it whilst waiting - a plan has a light at the end of the tunnel. If you are positive about your plan, enjoy the free things in life whilst waiting, then surprisingly your result may come sooner and unexpectedly.

There are lots of healthy, happy things we can do that are free - walk, visit a public art gallery or library, work on our self development, swim, help friends and neighbours on projects, watch birds or insects, take children to play in the park and many, many more. Also feel good about the confidence and faith your creditors had in you to allow you the debt level you have!

Just realise you won't need that consideration at the end of your plan because you will be free!

If it is a lousy job then make the best of it while you wait for your affirmation to work. Be visible so that someone can find you, to offer you another job, and do your existing job well and positively. No one wants to employ a negative attitude. Don't blame your existing job/boss - after all, no one forced you to be there but you! Take responsibility for your job and be positive no matter what - **Analyse, Centre, Reflect** - make a plan to move on and stick to it.

If your job is boring, use the time to work on development of yourself. Perhaps you might plan to get free of debt, save $10,000 and start your own business - layout the plan step by step and then start enjoying life away from work to the maximum – lift your energy level and time will fly as you race up those steps to reach your goal.

If you're subject to sexual harassment, but for some reason can't leave your job immediately, then take steps to minimise your exposure.

Wear looser, layered clothing that makes it more difficult to be touched. Turn it into a strategic battlefield and consider all the things you can do to avoid the issue. If it's possible to report it confidentially, or ask for a transfer, do so. Even a lesser job is better than one where you are harassed.

Many of you will think I should say report it immediately, or leave, but I am realistic enough to understand that some people are in a position where if they report it, or leave, they will be unable to feed their children next week. Everything is holistic.

If it is verbal harassment, centre and flow. Don't hear it as personal, but rather your positive energy can reflect it metaphysically back in the direction from which it came.

It may not surprise you now to learn that your positive energy can be so powerful, that the person harassing you simply stops and turns their attention to a weaker being - a classic victim.

It is probably appropriate in this category of Purge to take a quick look at what I call:

Classic Victim Syndrome (cvs)

Before I discuss this topic, I want to be sure you understand, I am not a qualified therapist but this is a condition I have identified in many of the people I have helped with my work.

I have also identified this condition in many, many people in the wider world that I meet and have discussions with. My research over several years has led me to conclude that this condition (syndrome) does exist and it would be great to see it recognized, and funded for research.

I suspect a solution, or even a better understanding of it, could positively impact a nations health bills. The great healer Louise Hay has done a lot of work in a related area, and I highly recommend her books.

I personally use her book Heal Your Body, every time I have pain, or a problem, or feel ill. I have found it one of the most powerful and useful books I have ever read, and it stays by my side and travels with me everywhere.

Classic Victim Syndrome

You will recall we talked about emotional crutches earlier in this section and we profiled "Charlie and Elsie" - all could be diagnosed with CVS.

CVS seems to be something we are not born with; we learn it from experience and conditions. Talking to psychiatrists, I have found this a largely unrecognized, unstudied condition, but it's often present from an early age. I have seen some very young children with CVS, but rarely treated holistically by the medical profession who continue to treat their symptoms. CVS is often, especially in children, initially caused by the actions of other, more dominant humans who are frequently sufferers of CVS themselves. CVS has, in my opinion, reached epidemic proportions in this world today.

On the next page I have outlined the most easily identifiable symptoms of a classic victim. These symptoms may also be caused by many other diseases, however a combination of these symptoms has shown me they are often a manifestation of CVS hidden undercover, which could arguably be a cause of the other diseases ability to manifest. For example, some of the conditions could be an indicator of drug abuse, but what is the underlying cause for the person to be substance dependant? I often see a classic victim present.

Classic Victim Syndrome:

Adult Symptoms	**Child Symptoms**
Sadness	Extreme mood shifts
Compliance and Resentment	Rebellion
Fatigue	Rejection of Values
Irritability	Irritability
Extremes of Weight	Extremes of Weight
Never Having Time for Self	Inactivity and
Fatigue	
Non-achievement	Bullying
Critical and Judgmental	Non-achievement
Low Self Image	Low Self Image
Nervous	Nervous
Fears and Phobias	Fears
Blames Circumstance for their position	

CVS Attracts These Conditions

Sympathy
Frequent Illness
Chronic Illness
Frequent Accidents
Work Obsession
Dominant & Controlling Partners
Violence
Robbery
Loss
Heavy Debt
Substance Abuse

Happily, CVS seems curable once a person is old enough to take self-responsibility. Sadly many can but do not choose to.

First, they must identify it in themselves, and whilst they may seek help, must understand that no one can fix it for them, the cure lies only within us.

Heartbreakingly, it is difficult to heal in young children as they do not have the depth of experience to work through the curative processes and frequently remain in the care of the causative factors, e.g. dominant or negative parents.

I personally have wondered how many weaker children die from illnesses that easily manifested because of the negativity and lower resistance induced by CVS before they reach an age where they can resolve it. I have met children, who due to adverse circumstances or negative outlook, have lost the will to fight even curable illnesses.

At the same time, I have met some kids who despite everything against them, they succeed and truly shine as beacons of possibility!

This serves as a strong reminder to all parents, that no matter how adverse your family or financial circumstances are, try to provide a positive and nurturing environment for your children. Allow them some suitable decision making for themselves as soon as they are able, do not dominate them, or try to make them to be as you wish them to. Allow them to be their own person and encourage them to grow in independence. Parents with independent children need not fear loneliness, especially if they follow this program themselves.

■

In many ways this book is indirectly about helping even mild victim syndrome, but there are some fantastic healers in the world who can do much more for advanced CVS than I can. See the Healing Section in my online book store www.terrieandersonstore.com

The Little Red Success Book is really written for the people who have already made a conscious decision to develop themselves.

An advanced sufferer of CVS would probably not have read this far or even bought this book because they would believe success was not for them, or believe the ideas in the book are selfish and cold. Still I believe it is important that we all recognise a CVS sufferer so that we can avoid giving out the sympathy which is the fuel to the syndrome's growth. Instead try empathy and a warm smile, encouraging them to view a more positive world. Above all, we must never abuse their generosity of energy, their bank is already low.

The first and only step to curing CVS is to recognise it and consciously commit to self development and change.

This is why it is very difficult for children to be cured.

From this commitment comes the strength, courage and resolve to break through into a new and more beautiful world. Then we accept responsibility for ourselves and our situation, and after which we develop self love, acceptance and approval so that the sympathy is no longer needed or even welcome.

When we remove blame and sympathy in our lives, we begin to be less critical, resentful and judgemental of others. We start to make time for ourselves, feel happier and begin to want to empower ourselves.

If you think you suffer from CVS, decide now if you should do some deeper healing before doing ARPIFEE. Judge this by how you feel about this book so far.

Step Four:

This is a more personal, inner step. It is primarily a result of all the other purging steps you are taking. So many people have told me "I can't do it Terrie, I feel so guilty".

Guilt is dangerous, insidious and a powerful negative emotion. You must begin now to forgive yourself for everything you feel guilty about in your life. The best way to do this is to go back in time and purge from the beginning.

Separate your life into periods, dependant on the amount of guilt you carry - if you were a really bad egg once, you may have to break it down into one year at a time!

Take a quiet, alone time - approximately one hour. Put yourself in a comfortable and relaxing environment, no loud or sudden noises or interruptions - this is very important. If possible have a mirror with you.

Firstly, centre yourself and feel at peace with your chosen environment. Then take a good look at yourself today - by now you should be truly beginning to love yourself, you are OK you know.

Say to yourself, "I am a good person, I love myself and I can forgive myself", preferably out loud. Now start off with that first memory and think slowly and deliberately through the period you have chosen.

Smile at the good memories, then when you feel embarrassed, shocked, dismayed or guilty at any memory, forgive yourself and anyone else involved for that incident, again preferably out loud preceded by the affirmation, "I am a good person, I love myself, and I forgive myself for .... "

e.g.

'I forgive myself for wetting the bed', breaking the window, hurting the sparrow, the frog, my friend etc.

If someone else was involved, who hurt you, then add "and I forgive ...(them)..... for (what they did to me).

e.g.

'I forgive my mother for hitting me when I wet the bed'

my father for not spending enough time with me

my friend for leaving me, etc.

Think about the incident, how important is it in your life today?

Maybe you need to verbalise your forgiveness, or express regret to the person involved to fully clear it. I

If so, do it as soon as possible, after the session. Do not go and throw yourself on the sacrificial altar, just use this for really serious guilt that you cannot just forgive yourself for. Go with humility, apologise and whether or not they chose to forgive you, leave with pride that you have resolved your guilt.

Then repeat that initial session to be sure that the guilt is truly gone.

Approximately 24 hours after a guilt purge for a life period, repeat the process of recalling the incidents, and see if the guilt is still there. You can try up to about three sessions, and if the problem remains, perhaps consult professional help. There are many types of therapy available. Personally I used kinesiology with great benefit and have seen it help others. One regretful word of warning, ensure any therapist is fully qualified to perform the services they offer - there are some, often well-meaning, poorly qualified therapists around.

Take the sessions for each period of time approximately one week apart. If you try to rush it, you will find it excessively draining on your energy level and not very effective, or lasting.

Be aware, serious problems such as incest, childhood violence and lack of affection can be far reaching and difficult for you to face alone, but help is available. If you can't purge something, it always seems to manifest itself in disease and disaster, and may even have much more serious consequences. If you have a problem of this magnitude, it is probably good to find a professional to help you rid yourself of the burdens.

What we want to achieve in working your way from apathy to ARPIFEE is a steady and pleasant personal energy level.

Step Five:

This is the final step in the purging process:

What is your physical lifestyle like?

Do you live in a fairly tidy, organised and uncluttered environment? Or is it a disaster zone?

Do you waste hours of your life looking for lost items?

Do you forget to pay bills on time?

Can you manage your cheque book?

Are you embarrassed if someone turns up unexpectedly?

Do you struggle to find clothes that are clean and ironed to wear?

If you were offered the chance tomorrow to move with a fantastic job in a week's time, could you do it?

To be happy and continue to be successful, we have to trust that the abundance of what we need is there for us - we do not need to hoard it.

To be happy we may wish to have many physical and creature comforts, and that is fine provided we adhere to three points:

1. We have what we need to do the things we most like to do regularly, in good clean working condition and where they can be located if we were suddenly blinded. (If you can only ski one day a year, hire the gear don't buy it!)

2. We believe that at any given moment in our lifetime if it became necessary, or desirable, we would part with these things, even without full compensation, without regret.

3. Caring for these objects does not prevent us from being free flowing, happy and successful, e.g. if you love gardening, but your garden is too big and creating stress - pave half of it and add beautiful pots and furniture!

If we become too attached to anything physical then immediately we begin to be restricted. Restriction causes frustration and stress which in turn becomes resentment, criticism and negative attitudes - the fast slide downwards.

To be happy, you must let go. If it takes you half an hour to lock up your house before you can go and enjoy yourself, and then you worry about it while you are away - either hire someone to care for it, or get rid of it!

You cannot be happy if you worry about your physical possessions. Take care of them, take the usual, normal precautions and then forget them. If someone takes them, or they vanish, then accept you are finished with them. This will be the hardest step you have to take in this whole course.

I still struggle with the weight of possessions and it is doubly hard, as in my case, where your partner cannot let go. My partner hangs onto a mountain load of stuff, in case we might need it - we rarely do! I desperately want to unclutter our lives because I feel constricted. It gets hard, so I ensure I regularly have a purge a few times a year.

It is a dynamic and final inner conflict for me, even today.

I have learnt to let go without distress, but have not yet completed purging out all the unnecessary in my life.

I have come to accept my partner will continue to stockpile his clutter. However I know - and he knows - one day, unless he lets go, he will miss a golden opportunity in life because he was too cluttered to flow.

There will likely be a few things in life that we do not want to free ourselves of, but as long as these things do not restrict you from the life you want to live and be happy, then that is fine. For me it is my teddy bear, he is very precious to me and been with me since birth, but he is also mobile and can travel with me anywhere, so he causes me no restriction.

Purging will continue to be a dynamic process in your life, as people and objects flow through your evolution. It is exciting, provided we don't clog up the exit - it is as important to let go, as it is to receive. I have started again, by choice, four times with no more than 2 suitcases, after having had a full house and all the desirable options one could want.

I found what I owned made absolutely no difference to my happiness or success!

This is a situation of true freedom.

What happens if I cannot purge an experience, or don't actually want to?

This question is so relevant and so important. I decided to move it forward into the main body of the text.

There is another technique that can be used here called reframing, or alternate reference. Let's say you have a friend that you really want to stay close to, but they are always upsetting you by making mildly destructive comments - perhaps jealousy. You have a choice through which window you view this friend.

The negative frame says "they are being bitchy, nasty, jealous etc" and you will suffer the downside of that view. It will probably cause you hurt and unhappiness. The positive frame says "The thing I like most about this friend is that they feel close enough to me to test my strength and beliefs". You will view the experience in a different light - we all need testing, and who knows if you change your response - they may change their approach!

A classic example of reframing was a friend of mine who lived in a suburb close to a large city. All the usual grit and grime abounded, but she had grown a lovely wee garden outside the kitchen. When I visited her one day, I was admiring the garden and wondered why she had a bright, checked curtain obscuring the top half of her outlook to this beautiful place she had created. She removed the curtain wordlessly, and I knew immediately. Without the curtain, one could see the smoke stacks of nearby factories and overhead telephone and power lines.

With the curtain in place the view was reframed and a totally, positive experience!

When I was young I was told I talked too much. Eventually a complexity of blocks was created by me around this belief. I avoided situations where I could talk much, and became quite shy of presenting my ideas and feelings. I could not purge this block without great difficulty, so I have given it alternative reference -

As a presenter, counsellor and writer, what better gift could I have than to be able to have enough to say! Imagine being on a podium with 5000 people listening and running out of things to say! This will never happen to me because I talk too much!

■

Key Notes - Purge

Purging, like reflection, is an ongoing habitual review of circumstances.

You must be in control of your life to feel successful.

Make the best of what you have while you're waiting.

No one wants to employ a negative attitude.

Guilt is dangerous, insidious and a powerful negative emotion.

To be happy and successful we have to trust that abundance of what we need is there focus - we do not need to hoard it.

To be happy you must let go.

IMAGE

Align yourself with power and you will have power,

Align yourself with failure and you will have failure.

.................Interpretation from Tao Te Ching

Image

Image is something to start working on once you have achieved two basics, first that you can now actually feel some love for yourself without embarrassment, second that you have begun, with some success, the purging process.

People often ask me "why can't I start on my image straight away?" It is actually very important that you don't!

Primarily we have to be fairly sure we know who we are and accept that person in the present, before we can decide what we want for our future.

If you think "I would love myself if only I had a smaller nose, or straighter teeth" then you don't have an image problem, you have a block from the past in your subconscious mind - purge it! If you were to have your nose surgically adjusted and your teeth straightened, it would cost you money, time, hours possibly weeks of pain and discomfort, then I can guarantee you that you will not have arrived at Nirvana! You will still have a problem, perhaps you will wonder who knows that you had surgery? What do they think? Should you have something else fixed?

If you purge properly first, you will probably decide you actually like your teeth and nose just as they are. They provide your uniqueness and after all this is just a brief physical evolution for the purposes of learning. In the overall infinity of time, does it really matter?

I don't have an issue with people wanting to adjust gross natural mistakes, or repair accidental damage, but to add poison to your face because you want to compete with a perfect 10, or to desire to look like someone else does not show a lot of love for who you are. I do believe cosmetic surgery is oversold to vulnerable people, and many of them are still not happy with the results, because the unhappiness is not reliant on the outside appearance. If you are happy and successful from within, you will have an almost magical glow that attracts fabulous people around you who believe you are beautiful.

By the end of this book, if you have followed the exercises, you will find success and happiness comes from within, and only from within.

To quote you a well known example, Mother Teresa of Calcutta did not present as a typically beautiful woman (she was a beautiful person, and she had that magical glow I mentioned above, but we are talking physical here), nor did she own very much, but from all I have read about her, she had a happy, successful and fulfilling life and without doubt she was incredibly powerful! She achieved fame and recognition, having never asked for it and without any pretentious ownership of any of the physical success trappings. I am not suggesting for a minute that we all want to be like Mother Teresa. Of course not, we couldn't be anyway. She, like all of us, is unique.

Success and happiness do not depend on any physical characteristics, or material possessions. They absolutely do not. However, it is important for normal mortals like ourselves, to be sure and confident about who we are, and what we want. This is where image comes in.

The type of image you desire for yourself must be achievable and comfortable for you to live within. It could be as varied as you can imagine, no image is good or bad, right or wrong, it is only what you choose for yourself. It will assist in your pursuit of success and happiness if you understand who you are, where you want to go and how you want to be. Understand though, your image will impact other people and affect the outcome of some situations, such as the business world where someone who wants to be a punk and a salesperson will have restricted opportunity.

As a guide, my image changed very little, but I went through a lot of experimentation to discover that much of the image I already had was actually right for me. It was a bit like trying on clothes -I took off what had always suited me and tried on a few other images! It was tough on my family as they went through not only changes in my dress and looks, but also the environment.

These are some of the challenges we faced:
- We moved house every 8-9 months.
- I changed my work.
- I bought and sold furniture.
- We went from vogue interiors to a mobile van.
- We moved from best suburb to fishing village.
- We tried living in city areas to country.
- We travelled from nation to nation.
- I tried heavy makeup and no makeup.

It was exciting, cost me a lot of money at times, and was sometimes stressful. The positive points were confidence; building on experience both work and life, I met truly wonderful, inspirational people, but above all had fun and adventure. The most positive point was that I now know who I am and that I am able to live in many different environments happily without losing myself.

I am no longer embarrassed when I look back at a photo because I will be as I am. I can now comfortably and confidently say 'I am what I am' and feel good about it.

My happiness, energy, and success still continues to grow daily.

I am not advocating that anyone else should go to that extreme; in fact hopefully many of you will be at this point today, more together than I was. I also did not find a simple, more general book that took a holistic approach to the topic - I waded my way through hundreds of books on varied topics and had to experiment on how to pull all this knowledge together simply, and in a way that was easy for me to work with, assimilate and apply in my daily life. I guess that is one of the main reasons I have written this book, to help you have a map to follow and get there faster and easier.

It may be that you already know that the image you have today is right for you and you feel good. Great! Don't change a thing, go to the next Chapter now!

If, however, you are unhappy with your image let's look at what you can do.

We must accept there are some things we cannot change, even if we desperately want to. We can't be a 6 foot hunk of blonde surf meat, if we are only 5.6," brunette and a weedy intellectual!

You can die your hair, build up your body, learn to surf and feel 6' but that is as close as you can get, and those dark roots will give you away every other week! (not to mention having to turn off the light when you remove your board shorts!) You would create an image recipe for disaster!

My advice is, within reason, try to accept your body as it is. It is only a vehicle on loan for this lifetime. Unless your body is in an unhealthy condition, don't waste energy and money making changes.

If you believe in reincarnation, order what you like next time round! For those who are disabled or suffering from any major physical affliction, then I ask you to also accept your body, love it and give it the utmost respect, it still keeps you alive Although there is no doubt that it may seem harder for you to be successful and happy, than for many others, you still can achieve it. Your body affliction may create an obstacle for you to overcome, but in doing so you will experience enormous spiritual growth and confidence. Based on my philosophy, I think you will be pleased that I have no sympathy for you, but empathy with your unpaved road ahead and praise that you have the courage to read my book and therefore the belief that you can be happy and successful. You are right, you can.

It may help you to daily search on the internet and read the many stories of disabled body people who have done truly amazing things and live very happy and fulfilled lives.

The only additional encouragement I can give you is that happiness and success are often the precursors of miracles.

We cannot change the past, our parents, family, past deeds and associations, our national origin, or birth religion. Accept the past, you must accept it and move on. Remember to forgive or rejoice, and walk forward. Your present and future are all you can change.

There are many things we can change - our respect for our bodies including how we dress them, what we feed them, how much we exercise, rest, suffer stress, and how we heal and love our bodies.

We can change where we live, how we dress, our environments, our type, or place of work, our personality projection, our friends and associates, pastimes, hobbies, activities, car, diet, religion, citizenship and a million other things about our physical life. Of course the most important change you are already making is on a metaphysical level, with your attitude to happiness and success. This is the change from within.

Everything we do, every day of our life, affects and projects an image. Not only to other people, but most importantly, to ourselves. If you consider yourself "down and out" today - you can change that by working on the image you project, and the image you feel. You will not attract success in your life if you continue to project the "down and out" image to others and to feel a loser yourself. You will find it hard to love and believe in yourself, if you prove to yourself daily that you are "down and out". I hate the term 'a battler' in life, we really don't need to 'battle' we need to project confidence, enthusiasm, happiness and be genuinely open to hearing opportunities to progress in the direction we want to go. If you are considered, or consider yourself, a battler – rethink this, why do you want to fight every day? Most happy, successful people do not fight every day, they live most days full of happy events, positive interactions and have great expectations. If you follow this program, and then continue to develop yourself, you will not need to be a battler and get sympathy business.

Generally if you consider that you are in a lower life position today, you will find two key factors in your life, dominance by others, and a lack of goals or plans. One important point to note - dreams are not, and must never be confused with, goals or plans. You must go through purging to get rid of those dominant factors in your life - this does not necessarily mean reject them, but rather learn to deal with them in a way to gain your own positive dominance. Then through analysis, reflection and focus set plans and begin to realise your goals, even bit by bit, this will be really uplifting for you. It is not very likely that you will go from street kid today to millionaire tomorrow, but you can do it over a few years. This may sound unbelievable, but it is true, and such progress has been proven by many. There are numerous poor, or ordinary, folk, who have acquired great success, and fame within a few years. Others who have achieved simple goals that allow them to live their lives the way they want, in contentment and happiness, they too are very successful human beings.

The key point here is that from wherever you are today on the happiness and success scale, it is an achievable and proven goal for you to reach above 95% success and happiness in your life - in fact, within a few years or less.

Image is both the signal, and the reward, of your quest to reach your goals. To begin to live your image before you achieve your goal assists you to feel more positive while you are getting there.

"OK" you say, "If am in debt and I need to purge that debt. I want to be wealthy and wear designer clothes, how can I start to live that image now?" Simple - first set aside in your plan a small amount of money for clothing, even whilst getting out of debt you must still be dressed!

Do you know how to look good and make the most of your image? Do you understand fabric and colour? If you do not understand these basics of good, stylish dressing, then find someone whose personal image you admire and ask them to help you.

Next, locate your nearest designer recycled stores – if you have a car, locate all the ones you could regularly visit. Now comes the fun, visit them regularly with a clear knowledge of your clothing budget and have patience - you will be very amply rewarded. One good designer jacket and two or three pairs of trousers (or skirts) is a good start. Who will notice budget tops and cheaper socks or stockings if the image looks Ace?

Believe me - no one will notice the cheaper bits!

If your budget is tight and you will not wear recycled, then look for budget lines that have look alikes for good designers, online stores are abundant in all major countries that specialise in this area.

In early years I had a funny situation. I had located a charity shop that the manager took a personal interest in. She seemed to find excellent men's clothing and my husband called in regularly.

Within a few weeks he had purchased a designer tag navy blazer for $25, 2 pairs of superb Swiss wool blend trousers for $30, a lovely leather belt for $2.

He also located a new pair of Italian leather shoes and a couple of silk ties. One morning at his work, a colleague commented to him "I don't know how you do it, we earn the same and you always look so fantastic, but I look like I've been dressed by Charity shops. "

We didn't forget this comment, because apart from the humour, some weeks later our son, who had continually tried to impersonate a giraffe in his early years, had grown out of his college trousers yet again after only 3 months.

We offered these trousers to this man for his son who was a year behind, on the basis it would be great to pass them onto someone who could use them (this was common practice amongst our friends and at the school). This man was horrified, he said he could not possibly ask his son to wear second hand trousers, even though he also admitted he could only afford the very cheap cotton drill ones. His son was not given the choice. So our son's expensive, long wearing wool trousers went to the charity shop that had helped us.

We have never refused anything offered to us; if we could not use it then we passed it on to someone who could.

This way the wealth of the world goes around. Once you are confident in yourself, it is as important to receive gracefully as it is to give.

Another example of this is cars. If your goal is to have wealth, and you want a wealthy image - do you choose to drive an obviously cheap car? An older prestige car at the time of writing costs about the same as a 5 year old small mass production car, so you must decide which car suits your image – a newer car of more common type or an older more prestigious brand car. Some people are influenced by the cars we drive, and will notice your chosen image! Either image is positive, but only you can decide which image is yours. The point is you have choices - we always have choice.

Live in an area that suits your image - it may be better to rent a cheap flat in a top suburb, than an average house in an average suburb – then again maybe where you live is not important to you, perhaps for example you want to travel so want to save as much as possible, that depends on what your image is!

Where you live and what you drive, even if you drive, and what possessions you have is totally dependent on the image you want to project and live. Be true to yourself, your goals may all be entirely non-material, and only achievement of those goals will make you successful! Don't get sucked into a lifestyle of the rich and famous if that is not consistent with your life goals. Do try though to make your lifestyle comfortable, as we all need a peaceful, safe haven to return to after a tough day.

All the facets of your life may need adjusting. I have one client who wants to have the reverse image, she is very wealthy, but wishes to have the image of a middle class woman because that is the social structure she feels most comfortable with. She flies economy, drives an average car, stays in 3-4 star hotels, wears production clothing and works as a secretary - but most importantly she is very happy. Much of her income is passed on as she sees fit, anonymously.

The most essential aspect is that all changes to image must be planned carefully, and implemented steadily to see how it feels; otherwise you'll become confused and have difficulty in establishing any image.

Just begin to live your goal, and taste it, from today on.

Good luck - I really enjoyed this image making but I made a few mistakes and had to backtrack! I also laughed at myself a lot through this time.

Key Notes - Image

Success and happiness do not depend on any physical characteristics, or material possessions. They absolutely do not.

Dreams are not, and must never be confused with, goals or plans.

Image is both the signal and the reward of your quest.

FOCUS

Maintain your position and you will achieve longevity.

..........Interpretation from Tao Te Ching.

Focus

If we have come this far together, on your second read through, we have probably been together now several months or even a few years! Depending upon how serious, and how strong you were through the hardest bits. Good News, I can assure you the worst is over and it gets easier from here.

We need focus now to grow from our recognition and acceptance of who, and what we are today, into what we have chosen as our ideal destiny. If we lose focus, I am sad to say it is almost a restart – so although you are now in mission critical and it is still a way to go, the need for keeping up is greater. To slip from here will undo much of your hard work and pain.

The good stuff is that you feel lighter, your life has less hassles, you can analyse and objectively chart your daily paths, you are experimenting with new forms of freedom, you are not too dependent on material things and you know and love yourself. In addition, you know where you want to go - now is the time to chart some longer distance miles.

One point, I will raise here, is that you may now be beginning to feel the first pangs of being alone; we will revisit this later, but be unafraid. It is normal and will increase, but you will handle it and even welcome it.

It helps if your partner is with you on this course because you can experience aloneness together and that is quite lovely. However, I have always walked this path alone and with a partner who does not embrace the program, it still works. They will enjoy your happiness and your success.

Focus is essential and is a key tool of planning. Never act on emotions, or fleeting thoughts, ever again. Always analyse - reflect, if necessary, purge, see if it fits your plan, then focus. No more rash judgements from here.

Focus is the most powerful tool we were ever blessed with. There is almost nothing it cannot do for you. As with all great power you must use focus with caution. If you were to focus on negativity, or evil, the effects could be catastrophic, and implosive to you.

Focus is the single minded determination that we put behind our efforts to achieve any desired objective.

Focus is available to us as an unlimited resource of power, it is free and depends only on our ability to use it.

Never struggle to achieve anything, put effort and focus to work for the shortest and least stressful route. Struggle is effort contaminated by emotion, exhaustion and pain. More on this in the next chapter.

Look at your goals to be achieved soonest, then greatest. If it helps draw a path like board game on a large sheet of cardboard, with start, and then place goals in order to reach final greatest goal at this time, as the "end" or "win".

Now focus on that first goal - what is the very first thing you need to do to get to it? Write it on the path and focus in real life on doing it. Everyday all your effort should be leading you, albeit maybe slowly, toward that first goal. If it is not, or worse still taking you away, then why are you doing it?

We should always write our main goals down on paper and place them where we can see them daily. Then before negativity sneaks in and disillusions us, we write on another piece of paper the actions we can take this week that will take us closer to our goals. We repeat this process every Sunday, having crossed off our actions as we achieve them. This way we feel successful every week and creep ever closer to our desired result.

We always realistically date our goals, so that we have a time frame to work within. My longest timeframe from conception was seventeen years and my shortest three months. Sometimes the final goals have looked ridiculous in their probable impossibility, but I have been totally successful in achieving my personal goals and Focus has always been paramount.

As an example, let us assume your goal was to buy a home in a suburb where you have always wanted to live, but believed you could not afford.

First, you might want to move into the locality where you want to buy.

What do you need to do to get there?

Save some money, or find a flatmate, or seek out the flat, or what?

Start doing it, and focusing your effort towards it every day. Each day, do at least one thing towards it. Put $5 in the bank and eat fruit for your lunch; or go meet a flatmate in that suburb; or walk in that suburb on Saturday and visualise yourself living there; join a community club there; shop there, tell someone you are moving soon; don't take that day off just to lie in bed; appreciate your job, (even if you don't like it) as it is helping you to achieve your goal. Focus on doing an awesome job, you may be promoted, or noticed by someone outside the Company.

I also now want to formally introduce the power of the focused affirmation. Affirmations are neat things but if they are random, irregular and or unfocused, they just create warm fuzzies!

You still need warm fuzzies, we all do, and there are some great and powerful, general affirmations you should be in the habit of using regularly by now, for just that warm, fuzzy purpose.

Focused affirmations are even more powerful. Think of them like light beams. The sun is wide and general with no focus, so the rays warn us and produce serotonin* helping us feel good. A laser is small but intensely focused, it can cut through steel, blast cancer cells.

- Great online article on health benefits of sun:

http://www.truestarhealth.com/members/cm_archives13ML3P1A21.html

This is about "laser" style affirmations. Let's go back to our example.

First stage new image, and move to better suburb in which we wish to ultimately buy our house.

A laser affirmation would be - "I deserve to live in x suburb". To be repeated frequently, in fact as many times as we remember each day. Then if we are walking the suburb, to "feel" our image and goals, try saying to yourself "I deserve to live here". "I deserve to live in a house like that one". "I am going to live there" etc. Never beg of yourself or question. your sanity E.g. Do not use "Please, I want to live here".. "I wish" "Please God" etc etc. - State your purpose, laser style without waver, feel it and believe in your own power of focus.

The same style of laser affirmation and focus can be applied to each step on your goal path.

When you are focused on your goal, question your important actions and decisions.

- Will they assist me reach my goals?
- Will they hinder me, or distract me from my goals?
- Does it fit in with my image of me that I find joy in projecting?
- Does it feel good and make me happy?
- Does it harm me in any way?

Get the gist? I am sure you do - sometimes I say "Yes" to neutral, fun things that although they don't assist me reach my goals, nor do they hinder me. They make me happy in the meantime and the waiting is easier.

Next go out and assertively claim your goals and directions. **You must be an active Universe participant to be noticed**. If you sit at home watching the soapies each day/evening because its cold, wet, hot, or you are tired, depressed or broke, then believe me your goals won't come and find you. You have to go hunting to feed yourself metaphysically. Make music and laughter; enjoy each day to the maximum.

Just remain focused with your eyes open and you'll see the opportunities offered to move forward, and if they fit, don't hesitate or they will be gone. Ask focused questions and if you get the right answers - go for it! Don't worry about waiting for everyone else to catch up, or approve - you'll miss the trip and sometimes it is many times harder to recreate it.

In particular, retain focus when people try to bring you down, or question, or laugh at you. Sometimes if I have a goal that is really important then I discuss the specifics of it with no one, but the Universe and myself.

I find this allows me to remain more powerfully focused. I then go about setting the climate for it to happen without hassle, and manoeuvring everyone, and everything necessary, into place for it to occur without harm or consternation for those near to me. Sort of prepare everything in the expectation of change that is coming. Sometimes this has been so powerful, my goal has been achieved much faster than I ever imagined possible! You need to remove all the obstacles and put in place, or motion, the events that make the achievements of your goal possible.

I once watched a small animal trying to build a nest in a stream. She kept bringing sticks and throwing them, only to wash downstream, in the flow – this went on for several days and I felt sorry for the lovely little animal.

Then I noted that the stream had slowed considerably and the nest was in progress - I realised all the sticks had piled up further along against some rocks and was slowing the flow down - I decided to assist and threw in a few extra rocks so that the stream slowed even more and diverted away from the nest area. I then realised that I should be more visionary and not feel sorry for the animal. She was creating the environment patiently, and with focus, for her miracle to occur. She even tolerated my presence undoubtedly more aware than I, that I would be the catalyst she needed eventually. I learnt a lot that week about the power of focus and persistence in achievement of goals and have used those lessons ever since.

Without focus you will expend enormous amounts of energy with little reward. Focus is a laser light, a truly powerful energy that can interact with the Universal energy needed to bring your goals to reality.

Focus can bring with it a feeling of aloneness, because it is a single-minded power. You can't really share focus. You can share an ideal, or a goal, with your partner and both agree to focus. Then it is back to each of you alone. If you try to focus together you'll get interference and judgement probably resulting in enmity. You should not even ask your partner how they are going - You focus on You and Your ability to focus! Leave your partner to their own best devices.

Envisage you are both saving to buy a new lounge - when you have the lounge, who remembers if one put in $50 more than the other? You have it, and that is what counts! You both achieved your goal!

Focus can also be an alone time because you may have to decline events, or social occasions, because they no longer head you in the right direction, suit your image or they may even hinder your movement. Perhaps some of your immediate pre-purging past life mates want to go on the usual Friday night pub crawl. You are saving to move to another suburb. So after you review the answers to the focus questions, and reflect, you might know something like:

- It will cost you your week's savings.
- It is very bad for your body and fitness
- These guys are a pretty negative lot
- The pubs they visit are in Down and Out land
- Last time you had to have a day off work

So you are alone on Friday night and they are all out having a "good time"- or are they? Where will they be in say 3 years time, when you have reached your goal?

Do something special instead - buy a chocolate and watch a movie! Go for a walk in the moonlight with the neighbour's dog! Visit another friend who may be alone, or cook dinner for them at your place!

Visit your intended new suburb, work on your car, do some purging, watch a good movie or get a book from the library - there are heaps of alternatives that you'll enjoy, keep you focused and leave you loving yourself even more!

Keep yourself aware, and reminded, of your goals and aspirations every day as much as possible.

This can be done many ways - pictures; your map chart on the wall; affirmations on the fridge, the toilet and as bookmark in your diary; detour through your aspired suburb to and from work, and feel what it means to live there, spend reflection time and watch these thoughts float past, allow yourself to visualise and fantasise about how you will feel, what you will see and do when you have achieved your goals. What you are doing is using focus to keep you reminded of why you are walking this particular path you have chosen.

Enjoy every minute of every day and let focus help you do that. Doing something short term, that used not to appeal, becomes more appealing when you stop hating or resenting your situation and view it differently. It has become just a temporary state needed to get where you want to go.

Here is an analogy for you. To see many of the most wonderful and awe inspiring views in the world you must sometimes experience discomfort, primitive transport and perhaps overcome fear.

The moment you see this view, you forget all the discomfort and feel the exhilaration! This high will last a long time, and recur every time you recall your experience - the trip to get there becomes something you laugh about later! Women will understand this same process with the miracle of birth.

Focus is of paramount importance as you climb to reach levels of attainment above the collective mentality. If you lose focus whilst climbing a mountain you are in danger of falling - the same applies metaphysically, it can also hurt and be hard to repair.

Focus is hard to learn, but it is possible and the rewards are infinite.

When you do learn to use focus effectively, you will experience awesome power, and astonishment at the feats you easily achieve!

■

Key Notes - Focus

Focus is essential and is a key tool of planning.

Struggle is effort contaminated by emotion, exhaustion and pain.

You must be an active Universe participant to be noticed.

You have to go hunting to feed yourself metaphysically.

Make music and laughter, enjoy each day to the maximum.

Focus is the laser light.

Enjoy every minute of every day.

Focus is of paramount importance as you climb to reach levels of attainment above the collective mentality.

EFFORT

Effort is of most value when timed precisely.

.... *Interpretation from Tao Te Ching*

Effort

Let's review where we are at today. After months of learning and exercising together we should now be feeling pretty light of head and experiencing considerable change in our lives. If not, please stop now and return to the beginning to start again. Tough call, but if you are on your second read, following the program then somehow if you don't feel the results you have missed something valuable along the way.

It is vitally important, before we look at applying serious effort, to ensure we have made it through to *focus* effectively and we now see major change in our attitude, and other peoples' attitudes to us. Otherwise it will be like a loaded machine gun in the hands of an untrained child - devastation in chaotic order, and total unpredictability in your life. You should be fully in control now, because effort is the live ammunition.

I am never sure in which order energy and effort should be taught because they go pretty much hand in hand. After many weeks of reflection, I am convinced effort should be first, but suggest you read these two chapters one after the other without the usual time periods of practice. Learn to use effort and energy together. As I mentioned in Focus, we don't want to struggle to reach our goals, with the natural Universal law in harmony it is relatively simple to reach them.

Most people in the collective mind talk about, and usually practise struggle. It is a human past time. Well trained mountaineers on a properly planned and equipped expedition don't struggle - focus, effort, energy get them to the top. In the event of crisis, only effort, energy and reflective analysis without emotion will ensure their survival.

Effort is the collective momentum, resources and focus that we place behind the wheel of day to day living that accelerates achievement. Effort is the antipathy of laziness. Lazy people will never reach long term happiness or success. There are two kinds of people who inherit, or win, money and then lose it. Lazy people and those who cannot see beyond struggle and the collective mind.

I have met many people who have gained a huge bonus, yet within two years have returned to the state they were in (or worse) before receipt of the bonus.

I met one couple who told me that they had received $1.2 million unexpectedly. At the time they fully owned their own average, suburban house (valued around $130,000) and owed about $500 on a credit card. They owned a car (not new but reliable) and were both in stable jobs. When they received their bonus, they lost all focus and direction. They indulged in dreams, fantasies and impulsive whims, including helping others that maybe were there to take advantage.

They told me they thought they were just lucky and did not reflect upon anything. When I met them they had spent the bonus, quit their jobs, lost their home and were quite heavily in debt.

Not believing their bad luck, it took quite a while for them to understand they were responsible for their situation. Riddled with criticism and resentment for those they had helped, they blamed each other and even their benefactor for giving them the money.

Additionally, their health suffered over this period.

We spent some time together. This couple chose to reframe, and change their attitude to, their situation. They commenced a plan to reverse their position and with focus, energy and effort they have succeeded.

Effort is clean, clear cut channelling of energy into a focused direction. Most importantly effort has no emotion and makes achieving goals seem relatively simple. Effort brings noticeable rewards quickly There is no room for pollution, with effort.

It is similar to leaving the city on Friday night, choked up with traffic, fumes, aggression and frustration, motoring out into the country, on and up a mountain range. You leave the car and walk maybe two or three hours to a cabin in the bush. When you wake up easily at sunrise, without alarm, and open the door you take a big, deep breath and exhilaration hits!

You take the axe and cut wood, whistling happily -
each swing cutting cleanly into the log. You feel so
good! Back in the city, colleagues of the collective
mind are struggling with dirty air, traffic, feeling tired
and needing material compensation, or worse, feeling
depressed. The key word is struggle. On the other
side, you are feeling fantastic, even though you have
to chop the wood before breakfast and it is freezing
cold. You are using "effort". Clean, pure, high energy
and positive effort.

Effort has to be focused at achieving our goals on a
daily basis. We have to make effort not to slip back to
our old ways, to eat correctly, not overindulge and to
do the things we need to do to reach those goals along
the pathway.

Every time you struggle to get the bus on time, you
have wasted valuable energy and lost focus about why
you are catching the bus. Maybe you need to purge
whatever it is that makes you late every day. My
example, I always thought I had low blood sugar in the
morning, and that was a great excuse to lie longer in
bed. I probably did have low blood sugar, after all - I've
been telling my body this for years - why wouldn't I?

Well, only very recently I realised I had another purge
to perform. I now remind myself every night before I
sleep, why I am resting my body. I rebuild the energy
ready to continue my effort tomorrow, to reach my
goals, and I am looking forward to the opportunities to

advance that tomorrow will offer. It works! I now not only sleep well, but I am waking refreshed and actually excited that it is a new day. I want to get up and often wake with one of my favourite affirmations on my mind. It feels fantastic!

I no longer struggle to achieve goals, to control myself or to be happy. I simply apply maximum effort to the daily objectives that assist me along my path. If I were to ever find myself struggling to do anything, I would stop and question my intention and whether I was doing what I should be.

Strugglers seem to battle on forever getting tired, being victims and receiving little more than sympathy. Anyone I meet who tells me they struggled to be where they are today is usually quite embittered, resentful, easy to anger, or demanding and demeaning of others, and often they are victims, or alone. They rarely have total happiness. The same as the people who spend many hours describing to all who will listen how hard they work, instead of struggling so hard, they could use that time to relax or even apply effort to their goals. They are unhappy.

When you are feeling good about yourself it is far easier to achieve anything, because you commit effort and focus to your daily activity. You gain great joy from almost anything you do and if you don't want to do it, you are strong enough to say no without fear.

I believe it is appropriate again here to remind you that you will be beginning to feel more distant from many people, and often more alone (in your head). This is because you know so much more than most of those around you, and you begin to see them and their daily activities quite differently.

This is very normal of course as you are becoming an achiever and happier. You have chosen this path to success and that automatically makes you one of a minority group. However, on a positive note you will also begin noticing your own impact on others, and that some people stare at you, or seem to go out of their way for you. Remember that special glow I talked of earlier? Well it's beginning to be very visible. You will feel special – it is OK – you are now very special. You will already be an inspiration to many people you know, or meet. Be aware, some people close to you may feel some negative feelings such as loss at having to share you, or even jealousy; they may often unintentionally try to bring you down again.

You will have already experienced a huge increase in your own energy and personal contentment; you will feel excited with anticipation of what is to come. It was at this stage I began to feel confident inside, rounded and complete, approving of myself. No straggling bits of me trailing behind, to snag on the bushes beside my path.

A good friend of mine is a very successful and happy man, and he calls his philosophy 'one minute more'. He said 'I spend one minute more with every person I meet. It makes me feel better and contributes to my success.' He is absolutely right, anyone who meets him never forgets him. Interestingly, I have noticed that many powerful people remember him and make time for him, despite the number of people they meet. He has charisma and a sense of magic about him.

Continue to make the effort to love yourself, and those you meet, each day. It has great impact!

■

Key Notes – Effort

Effort is the collective momentum, resources and focus that we place behind the wheel of day-to-day living that accelerates achievement.

Effort is the live ammunition

Effort is the antipathy of laziness

Effort is clear, clean and channelling of energy into a focused direction

Effort has to be focused at achieving our goals on a daily basis

Make the effort to love yourself, and those you meet, each day.

Effort has great impact!

Try and give everyone you meet 'One Minute More'

ENERGY

Accumulating energy makes all things possible, thus your potential is unlimited.

...............................Interpretation from Tao Te Ching

Energy

This is one of my favourite topics on which to write and talk.

Energy is exciting and it is fun. It is still not easy to start, but I can reassure you it gets easier as the months roll by! Automatically, due to the fact that you feel lighter, happier and your goals are becoming closer, you will be experiencing a lift in energy.

Energy is the performance characteristic of every individual and it can be tuned just like a high performance engine to peak perfection. Just like a high performance machine it can also break down if it is not maintained, or skid off the track if we let our attention wander. So once we get our energy levels rising, it is increasingly essential to keep focus.

Otherwise you will be like a spinning top fascinating, fast but going nowhere at a dizzy pace until you fall exhausted.

As your energy lifts, you will be tempted at first to try to do too much. Remember the higher your energy level, the further you have to fall and the more it hurts. So greater attention must be paid to diet, sleep patterns, environmental exposure, purging (to ease the load) and focus.

Also always keep a new goal in front of you. The lack of a goal is the fastest shortcut to total energy loss that I can think of.

Energy cannot be stored for long, it must be continually replenished. Boxed up energy usually turns to frustration, so we need to generate and use it daily. Let's now look at ways that we can lift our energy and some examples of how to use it.

Sleep

Sleep is the natural body, mind and soul reviver. I won't talk too much about the metaphysical benefits of sleep, as I promised I would keep this book really simple. The average adult needs around 6-8 hours daily sleep, with no more than about 16 hours between sleep periods, on a regular basis. This is a healthy pattern that provides opportunities for healing, rebuilding of energy reserves, and rest from the effects of light and radiation bombardment.

Another important aspect of invigorating sleep is to have fresh air, so if your apartment is air conditioned, open a window anyway! If you live on a main highway - move someplace quieter and with cleaner air as soon as possible, but in the meantime filter your air through the window. There are many inexpensive ways to achieve this. To gain energy from sleep, we must have fresh air and minimum amounts of electromagnetic radiation (EMR).

If you have an electric blanket, get rid of it and use a hot bottle - or at least turn it off before you get in the bed! If possible, secure some soft music that you really like (there are lots of great New Age musicians) and play it while you prepare for bed and up until you sleep. It is very soothing and relaxing.

Ensure that whatever you read or hear, before sleep is positive food for your mind and soul. Murder mysteries are definitely out, if you immediately have to sleep afterward! I strongly recommend against watching TV just before sleeping - it is very questionable behaviour. You are handing control of one of the most important parts of your day over to a Program Manager you probably don't even know!

Before going to sleep, it is really good to meditate, or at least just sit quietly (with straight spine, eyes shut) and watch the thoughts of the day float out, without attachment, past you and away. Try those centering and reflecting techniques we discussed earlier in the book.

If you wake during the night and have difficulty going back to sleep, then begin all the techniques that are listed above including some of your favourite affirmations. Never struggle to sleep! It is useless thrashing around getting annoyed. You will find as you use these techniques, and your energy level lifts, that your sleep patterns become an easy fit in your lifestyle, and you will awaken refreshed and excited about the new day!

Environmental Influences

Everything, and everyone, around you has the potential to affect your energy level. Some people are just like sponges, in that, they have an unquenchable thirst for draining the energy of others.

I had friends like that - always with a problem, lives full of self-induced negativity. I used to become involved, try to assist in a meaningful way and come home myself exhausted and irritable not even fully realising why. "Had" is the essential difference!

An important point to understand here is that your subconscious mind cannot distinguish between reality and fantasy. What you witness, or think, (therefore watch on a screen, or read) is real to your mind.

That is why you cry in a sad movie, or cringe in a terrifying one! You know consciously they are only actors, but your subconscious mind does not! This is a very significant point and should ring warning bells for you.

The type of material you read will affect your energy level. If you only love horror, murder, intense, intrigue or pornography - go back to analysis, reflection and try some purging. Ask yourself why you want to read, or watch, death, destruction and fear. Generally, it has to do with raising your adrenalin levels and feeding the collective mind gratification in the need for fear. Some people can read horror and remain detached, if you have this skill, then the choice is yours.

Let's talk about fear. Why do we feel fear? It is conditioning from early childhood. All our lives everyone we trust has constantly reminded us by voice, or force, of all the things we cannot do. So we have learnt fear better than almost anything else, usually second only to guilt!

Fear is nothing but a belief in the possible reality of our own thoughts. We fear what may happen, but because it has not happened, we are actually fearing our own thoughts. Incredibly silly really, isn't it? We will look at fear again in the questions section at the end of this book.

If we learn not to fear, then suddenly the movie makers and writers who are purveyors of fear and destruction to meet the demands of the collective mind, no longer receive our support. If you ever want to see the effects of fear - take a look at the lives of many of the Hollywood Stars! Success without total happiness is short lived. Many stars who made millions and had powerful friends, end up penniless and alone, or die early in despair!

It is essential, to protect your energy levels, that you strictly sensor your own input - what you watch, read and participate in. There isn't even much good news on the evening news program - try reading the paper at least you can choose what you need to know!

Alternatives are abundant to watching negative TV programs, or reading negatively focused stories about "drama in real life". (Real life can actually be quite peaceful and not dramatic if you accept it to be that way.) Try watching, or playing a sport. Your adrenalin will still flow but with positive enjoyment. Try reading a heart warming novel or a self improvement book, you can just sit and reflect - an hour will pass quickly and unnoticed. Go for a walk, do some floor exercises, join a dance studio or gym, take up a new hobby, research a topic, go to dinner with a friend - the list of positive activities is limited only by your imagination

One thing I like doing is spending quality time with my friends and learning much more about how they think about life. Just ask open questions and listen, it is very interesting and will bring you much closer together.

Diet

It is very important that you ensure your diet is right for you. There are a few basic guidelines I can give you, but if you really want to find the right program (particularly important if you have a weight problem either way, or cravings) then make an appointment with a dietician through your nearest healing clinic.

Some basic guidelines are to limit your intake of fats, sugar, processed foods and cooked food. You need protein but don't overdo it. Be careful not to eat too many vegetables of the brassica family (broccoli, cauliflower etc) in any one day. Sugar and fat, in my mind are the really destructive foods along with processed food and anything that has spent too long encased in plastic or Styrofoam or been sprayed to hasten ripeness.

If at all possible grow your own herbs, even as pot plants - at least you can supplement your cooking with totally organic herbs.

Another basic idea that I can pass on is the recommendation for a good balanced meal. Check the table below. Each meal should in part, contain a combination of A+B or B+C never A*C. This ensures each part of the meal is complimentary and provides the fibre, protein, amino acids and complex carbohydrates we need for good health.

Group A	Group B	Group C
Grains	Legumes	Nuts
Cereals	Soy Beans	Seeds
Pasta	Peas	
Wheat	Beans	
Bread	Lentils	
Muffins	Raw Vegetables	
Biscuits	Steamed Vegetables	

Avoid excess, at all costs, of everything. No clarification needed here, just do it if you want balance and harmony in your life. Personally I have found that excess anywhere in your life throws out the balance. It is better to eat five small meals with exercise between, than to eat three large ones.

It is better to really savour the occasional glass of superb wine, expensive champagne or favourite drink than to go to excess, or habit, with alcohol. I have favourite champagne that I have an occasional bottle of and I love vintage red wine. So rather than ban these from my life, I really enjoy them in moderation and only now and then. The harmony remains.

Eat lots of fruit and vegetables for both the water base and the fibre. A great day starter is to have fruit at breakfast, as often as possible. As fruit is digested beyond the stomach it is always best to eat fruit first - it is a great cleanser to allow full enjoyment of the food tastes to follow.

Music

Of all the energy environmental factors this is absolutely my favourite. Music is a series of frequency tones that are put together in a pattern - music is actually just noise! Ideally you need balance here. Let's say you are a hard rock fan - well the good news is I want you keep enjoying it! The bad news is I want you to start mixing it with the antipathetic alternative -

soft, soothing music. Start off before bedtime by using the soft sounds to wind you down. Hard rock has an adrenalin producing effect that can be very destructive, it can cause you to feel aggressive and produce high negative energy levels. I am a rock music fan and it used to be 90% of what I listened to. Now by evolution it is about 10-15%. By choice, not conscious decision. Let's look, as examples, at the possible positive and negative effects of some other types of music on our moods:

Country & Western

- Often sad, lonely, broken hearted, sense of loss. Many doey-eyed singers with long faces and lean bodies.

+ Homely and comforting - easy to hear.

Jazz-fusion

- Can be out of balance, unstructured, sometimes irritating as the body likes rhythm and pattern.

+ Often played by eccentric, unique individuals. Clever, creative and stimulating.

Blues

- Again a sense of loneliness but not so desolate. Dramatic if it strikes personal emotional keys. Very dependent on lyrics.

+ Calming, laid back and not too intrusive.

Ballads

- A mixed bag, even on one album, of the above. A lot of real life drama,

+Often relaxing, gets you into a groove, a sense of fun.

Classical

- Usually historical, occasionally adrenalin pumping, sometimes very depressing.

+ Highly structured, disciplined, high skill levels required, feelings of opulence as traditionally associated with the rich. Can be uplifting.

New Age

- Can be boring, often lacks stimulation, unusual instruments.

+ Composed and played by a wide variety of people. Relaxing, calming, uplifting if played appropriately.

World Music

- Can be discordant with your culture, sometimes irritating

+ Diversity is a growth element, can be very relaxing or stimulating, fun producing. Often comes from grass roots of culture.

There is room in this world for all music, and if heard in balanced way there are only positive types of music. I enjoy all of the above music at different times. I will probably have a lot of angry musicians writing to me to defend their bent, but I can only question why they are angry? Is it fear that I may be right? Or fear of something else? We only assume defensive action when we are afraid. If there is no fear then defence is unnecessary.

What I am proposing to you is that you understand clearly the effects of noise, including music, around you and regulate what you hear to meet the needs of yourself. Practise diversity to suit your mood and needs.

Music, particularly, produces emotional change – a world without music for me would be a silent hell. Make it work for you in a totally positive way.

Incidentally, if you suffer deafness, play music anyway as the vibration of sound waves will still affect your body. Feel the speaker vibration with your hands. Ask a friend to dance for you, that you may visualise the music.

Early in the morning (that I now enjoy) I would want nothing to override the sound of the dawn chorus of birds near our home. It is so wonderful just to sit in the early morning sun and hear them sing while I reflect upon my new day.

It's challenging if you have a partner who likes a clock radio to waken them. Try giving them a small personal radio they can carry about, and asking for a compromise with a different alarm. In the meantime you must accept their needs and wait to celebrate a new awakening that will often come.

Incidentally, that is one of the great joys of a partnership in life - watching the other partner develop as a consequence of your quest, and the change in your attitude, is like a perfect rose opening slowly each day. It is the joy of knowledge that you have unobtrusively contributed in the most positive way possible, to the evolution of the person you love most, after yourself.

Sunshine - Fresh Air

Both of these are important factors in sustaining your energy levels. Chemically these environmental factors have a major impact on your body's well being. Fresh air is the only thing that is an exception to the excess rule - have as much as you possibly can. Sadly due to fellow man's disregard for our environment the sun must now be treated with caution. It is so good for us but we must protect our skin from burning. Take all the recommended precautions for your skin type and protect your eyes from glare. However, no matter how low you are feeling, a walk in the fresh air and sunshine will lift your spirits.

If you live where you cannot access fresh air, may I suggest you invest in an air purifier so at least you breathe cleaner air at home. Or fill the house with lots of Madonna Lillies, the clean air plant.

Activity Levels

Energy feeds on energy, so although you need quiet rest periods to meditate, reflect, sleep and just plain relax, these should be in perspective. In a 24 hour day we need 6-8 hours sleep, 2 hours for meals, 1 hour for bathing and other bathroom activities, that leaves us with at least 13 hours. On an average day a minimum of I0 hours should be spent with higher activity levels.

Work, sport, hobbies, real mental stimulation, exercise and fun should easily fill these hours.

Sometimes you might just take a whole day out, dedicated to relaxing, because you have 'pushed ' it all week long. Preferably these days of "full on" or "full off' should be the exception.

A healthy body and mind enjoys some amount of regular, balanced behaviour and input rather than a totally chaotic lifestyle. This doesn't mean you have to have a routine, or be boring, but ensure that every day maintains its balance. If you have a particularly stressful day at work, ensure you plan a particularly calming evening for balance. Reflect upon and purge the stress. Remember you no longer "have" to do anything, so you are free to change plans if you need to, so that balance is restored. Your happiness must be paramount in your life for total success. Sounds selfish but you should know by now that it is all OK.

You are in control of your life now.

We have but touched on a few of the important ways to preserve and increase your energy levels.

Energy is the momentum behind effort. The higher your energy levels are, the faster you will achieve your goals. In turn the more confident and self-loving you become, you will look to greater goals and you will find yourself feeling fantastic. Life Will actually get better every day, hurdles and trials appear smaller (that yesterday may have seemed insurmountable) and those people around you will seem nicer.

When you began this course if you saw a garbage tip you felt bad, but now you will start to see the birds that feed from it instead. You will continue to have a new vision of the world in which you live, and when ARPIFEE becomes a lifestyle, you will want to explore greater and more amazing paths that are available. Believe me, when I tell you this is just the kindergarten "you ain't seen nothin' yet!"

To continue even as you are, you must guard those energy levels carefully - they are the key to success in the program. When you feel so good, if you allow yourself to slip back you will feel worse than ever before, because you are no longer familiar with low energy feelings, situations or moods.

Low energy days are when you will have accidents, allow sickness in, lose control, or worse, give up the path you have chosen. When you find yourself facing a low energy day - first accept you caused it and don't blame anyone else! Then fix it immediately you become aware of it. Do whatever you need to do as a matter of urgency because you will not be in control and be placing yourself at risk.

Like driving a car, once licensed you have a responsibility to yourself and others. A course in success and happiness places upon you a special licence to affect the lives of others and control of your own.

■

Key Notes - Energy

Success without total happiness is short-lived.

Fear is nothing but a belief in the possible reality of our own thoughts.

We have learnt fear better than almost anything else, usually second only to guilt!

Avoid excess, at all costs, of everything.

A world without music would be a silent hell.

A walk in fresh air and sunshine will lift your spirits. If there is no fear then defence is unnecessary.

AFTER ARPIFEE

Powerful people can enter the whole, not simply the exterior. They occupy reality and ignore pettiness.

...........Interpretation from Tao Te Ching

After ARPIFEE

Well, we have finished this first long and perhaps difficult path together and I hope you feel the journey was worthwhile. I know it can be. If you really took this lifestyle on board you will feel very special today.

What happens from here -

l. Never stop setting goals and achieving success and happiness, you can always slip back to the collective mind unawareness.

2. Those of you who bought the book and don't know why - put it on the shelf with all the other similar books you believe didn't work and wait for another time.

3. Remember whatever you believe you are, you will be. Show love, for yourself everyday

4. Repeat affirmations every day, many times if possible.

5. Keep on Analysing, Reflecting, Purging, Focusing and applying Energy and Effort - they are all dynamic functions of your new lifestyle. (Check your image occasionally as well!)

6. Meditate regularly. You may find your Source, and great peace.

7. Smile often and enjoy the simplicity and beauty that surrounds us.

8. Have fun and enjoy your life. Travel and spread your happiness and success.

9. Maintain your balance of everything – no excess.

10. Read, listen, enquire and discover more - there is much more, this is only the beginning.

The biggest mistake most of us make, is it works so well we stop doing it! This is a big, easy trap waiting for us, don't fall in it!

ACCEPTANCE

Avoid interference and you will be able to respect life

.... Interpretation from Tao Te Ching

Acceptance

Acceptance was going to start off, or even be the subject of, a new book - it is so important. However, I felt it would add to the possibilities of success and happiness to include a brief overview on acceptance in The Little Red Book.

Acceptance is like a regulator, and with practice assists enormously in control of negative emotion. It also helps regain your equilibrium if you do lose it, occasionally. Acceptance becomes your rational control knob!

Fine, you say but what is acceptance?

It is the exercising of positive choice to accept the things in life that we cannot change, without causing ourselves unhappiness. Many people only see life as winning or losing, so if on average you lose a lot you will feel pretty bad. To me this idea now seems like seeing life in only black and white - without colour, how drab and sad!

Acceptance is the soft colours in our lives.

Acceptance is also the loving of someone as they really are - warts and all! You can offer positive influence, and example, but if that is ignored then your choices under win/lose are pretty narrow. You can reject them or embrace them, or worse destroy your happiness trying to change them!

Accept responsibility for yourself, your actions, the resultant consequences of those actions and of everything that happens to you.

Heavy stuff I know but a total acceptance of everything pertaining to oneself does two things.

First, it places the responsibility with the only person who can change your true happiness level. YOU. Second, it prevents you blaming everything else including, in some cases, inanimate objects (that damned nail sticking out of the wall!) and laying liberal mounds of guilt around, affecting others.

Now you are more aware, you have a greater responsibility not to worsen the evolution of others and the chance to expand your own evolution.

I have several friends who like to hunt animals for sport. I do not like that facet, or action, of my friends. They know I do not believe they should kill animals for sport, but they do not agree.

I have some choice - I can be unhappy, feeling negative towards them, even try to change them. I can pretend it does not matter; I can stop being their friend or I can accept that I do not like their action, but it is part of them so I accept the friends as they are - because I view them from acceptance. The other values and qualities that made them dear to me remain so. I do not go hunting with them. I do not share the experiences and I do not discuss their weapons. I also do not lay guilt upon them because why should I judge their action? In time that just becomes a part of them that does not appear to me.

In acceptance, we must learn not to judge. After all what is it to do with us, if they are "wearing that dress again" or "cheating on their wife" or any other thing that really is none of our damned business!

Judgement = Negativity = Unhappiness

Every time without qualification!

Judge only what is right for you to do, and feel, and say, and have, and wear - let others do the same.

I particularly hear judgement at times of drama and crisis. Society, the tribe, has expectations that everyone else's behaviour should be traditional, or what they expect it to be!

When I was a child I used to hear "they say ...." a lot - but no one could ever tell me who "They" were! Let us look at a few examples.

Funerals:

Do you have to go? Wear black? View the body? Cry?

Have one yourself? Does anyone else?

Weddings:

Do you have to be a virgin? Wear white? Marry in a church? Invite your mother? Invite your in-laws? Tell your friends? Does anyone else?

Dinner:

Do you have to take wine? Take flowers? Arrive on time? Take a partner? Go alone? Does anyone else?

No! No! A categorical No! Some things may be more polite, makes others feel respected, but they are not forced on you.

You don't have to, unless you want to – neither does anybody else.

I usually try to arrive on time out of respect for others, but if I am unavoidably late I also expect understanding, it can happen to all of us.

If people don't respect your right, that is just a matter of lack of acceptance. So many people make sacrifices of themselves because no one else is doing the "right thing" How crazy!

I heard a story today - a woman recently died. The brother who lived some distance away was moving house and said he could not go. The sister from another state had been very ill and did not feel well enough to travel. The third sibling lived overseas and was not coming back to the funeral. When the sister found out, she became upset and angry and so she flew to the funeral. Everyone in the family became involved in what was now a doubly negative experience.

The guilt, recrimination and judgement was thick in the air!

If you don't want to go to a funeral, even if it is the closest person to you - don't go!

More importantly if someone else doesn't go, and you do - just accept their decision as right for them.

Sometimes it seems like we "had" to inconvenience ourselves so we 'judge" that so should everyone else!

Acceptance of others and the way they behave is a very special way of strengthening and focusing on yourself - after all, you are only responsible for you, no one else.

I often observe that people who are not in control of their own emotions and lives are the ones most interested in trying to control the lives of others.

Accept yourself as who you are, mould the inner person from within to be who you want to be.

Rejoice in that self awareness and feel your own happiness grow to the point where you can accept those things and people around you as they are. If you don't like what you see, go somewhere else where you do like it, or at least can accept it.

The payback for acceptance, apart from your own happiness and flow of life, is an incredible inflowing of love and delight from all directions. People will be attracted to you, and you will see beauty where once you saw despair!

This is not an easy technique to master, start with one area of your life, practice until you have it and move on to the next one. Remember piece by piece!

■

Key Notes - Acceptance

It is the exercising of positive choice to accept the things in life that we cannot change.

Judge only what is right for you and let others do the same.

You don't have to, unless you want to - neither does anyone else.

You are only responsible for you, no one else.

Questions Many Have Asked

1. *How do I overcome fear?*

Understand and accept we experience fear because we are in our ego.

Understanding that fear is only thoughts of the unknown, or the possible. Once an event actually occurs, that fear is usually no longer present. If it is, it is further thoughts of the unknown or possible, new fears.

Accept that these are only thoughts, and learn to control them with unemotional detachment. This will become easier to do with practise

An additional method of handling fear is to write down a plan of what you would do in the event your fear occurred. Once you have a plan, you will feel more in control.

I knew a lady who lived her days afraid that "something" would happen to her husband, always worrying away at the back of her mind. If he was late, she feared that things had occurred to him. Nothing did until he was 75, and died suddenly of a heart attack right beside her! She had missed many years of total happiness over thoughts of events that never came to pass!

How much better those years could have been for both of them? Imagine the additional wonderful, happy memories she would have had to sustain her!

If you are afraid of flying, the reality is fear of crashing, injury and death - not a fear of flying! It is the same with every fear; it is just thoughts of a possible outcome or event.

Meditation will help remove the fear of death. As that is most often the ultimate fear, this will aid the control of many other fears. One last comment. The more you fear something, the more likely you will be using negative power to create the very thing you fear!

As a note of sanity, I am not talking about the fear that you would have if someone has a gun at your head, although the fear is the same (you are afraid of being hurt, dying etc) there are very few people who can control fear at such a time of real and immediate danger. Of course, the more you can hide your fear and appear calm the less you will agitate your predator, they often feed on the energy from your fear, it is their satisfaction.

In this book we are talking about controlling everyday fears and concerns that are not an immediate danger to anyone.

2. How do I stop feeling guilty?

Purging will remove most of your guilt.

Then by loving yourself, you will find less need to feel guilty. If, however, you continue to struggle with either purging or guilt, I would recommend a visit to a qualified, well trained kineisiologist.

Incidentally, they can also help enormously with deep seated fears. Do not let guilt fester. Along with hatred and resentment it is one of the most destructive emotions possible, both mentally and physically.

Guilt seems to be one of the most difficult factors we need to face when trying to be more happy and successful than the average person. It is the weapon used by most people to control others. We must learn to clear the weight of guilt, as it is too heavy a load to carry.

Final Word

I hope you have enjoyed our journey together as much as I have enjoyed writing and sharing the program with you. I do know that these principles work if you apply them every day, and a small reminder: whatever you do - if it works for you – don't stop doing it!

This is the biggest single point of failure that many people and businesses arrive at. Something works so well that they forget to keep doing the very things that made them successful!

If you check my website http://www.terrieanderson.com you will see that you can subscribe to various support updates if you wish.

Should you wish to contact me please use the 'Email Me' link on www.terrieanderson.com

Wishing you Success, Happiness and a life fully lived,

Terrie

http://www.littleredsuccessbook.com

http://www.terrieanderson.com

http://www.trulygreatleadership.com

Other Material from Terrie Anderson

30 Days of Inspiration is truly an amazing book, due for release November 2009. In just 30 Days Terrie can help you change the way you live your life, and give you more free time, a sense of control and set you up for a successful profile. It is great addition and support to The Little Red Succcess Book.

You can buy it as a small book to keep by your side, or you can enrol in the 30 Day email program online at www.littleredsuccessbook.com.

Either way you choose to participate, this program has had outstanding success.

The Essence of Truly Great Leadership is a coaching course for people seking to become leaders of excellence. It can be completed online or inhouse. www.trulygreatleadership.com

Free video presentations can be found on YouTube.

You can google Terrie Anderson for even more links.

Free Articles, Blogs and other helpful material can be found on all of Terries websites.

Highly recommended is the **Free Membership**, on www.terrieanderson.com as it will keep you posted on new books, articles, videos and other work by the author.